SURVIVING AS A
MIGRANT
WORKER
IN THE GREAT DEPRESSION

A HISTORY SEEKING ADVENTURE

by Matt Doeden

CAPSTONE PRESS
a capstone imprint

Published by You Choose, an imprint of Capstone
1710 Roe Crest Drive, North Mankato, Minnesota 56003
capstonepub.com

Library of Congress Cataloging-in-Publication Data is available on the Library of
Congress website.

ISBN: 9781669058137 (hardcover)
ISBN: 9781669058106 (paperback)
ISBN: 9781669058113 (ebook PDF)

Summary: YOU are struggling to survive during the Great Depression. As a
migrant worker, you travel from place to place hoping to earn enough money to get
by. How will you find a way to feed and clothe yourself and your family? Step back
in time to face the challenges that real people were met with during this difficult
time in history.

Editorial Credits
Editor: Mandy Robbins; Designer: Heidi Thompson; Media Researcher: Jo Miller;
Production Specialist: Tori Abraham

Image Credits
Alamy: Ana Rocio Garcia Franco, 71, Heritage Image Partnership Ltd, 12; Getty
Images: Archive Holdings Inc., 100, Bettmann, 30, 39, Buyenlarge, 61, Fotosearch,
103, Historical, 20, 23; Shutterstock: Daniel Reiner, 96, Everett Collection, Cover,
18, 35, 49, 58, 65, 83, Jesus Cervantes, 90, Noelle D. Gallant, 42; Superstock: Circa
Images/Glasshouse Images, 56, 77, Image Asset Management, 53; Wikimedia:
NARA, 4

TABLE OF CONTENTS

ABOUT YOUR ADVENTURE

YOU are living through a difficult time in U.S. history. Dust storms rage across the Midwest and South-central United States. The economy is in ruins. Jobs are scarce. People struggle just to eat. You're on the move, without a permanent home, in a constant search for work.

Bring the past to life as you join in the struggle to survive as a migrant worker during the Great Depression. YOU CHOOSE which path to take. Will you prosper? Or will you fall victim to the hardships that await you?

Turn the page to begin your adventure.

CHAPTER 1

ON THE MOVE

Your boots are worn. Your feet are blistered. A layer of dust covers you. Your stomach rumbles, and your pockets are empty.

It's the early 1930s, and times are tough. The wealth and prosperity of the 1920s has come crashing down in a big way. An economic collapse called the Great Depression has hit. Farms and businesses are failing. Millions of people are out of work. The stock market is in ruins. It is the basis of the American economy, where investors buy and sell shares of companies. People from all walks of life are paying the price.

Turn the page.

The economic collapse is only part of the problem. Severe dust storms have only made matters worse. Most of the country's heartland is in the middle of a disaster called the Dust Bowl. Years of planting crops in one place for too long has stripped the land of its topsoil.

Great clouds of dust kick up over the once-thriving farmland. As crops fail, farmers are forced to flee their homes. Like you, they're all looking for work. Any job will do. You just want to earn enough money to make it through another day, week, or month.

Not long ago, you had a comfortable home. You weren't rich, but you had enough money to get by. Food, clothing, shelter—you took all of the basics for granted. Not anymore. Like countless thousands of others, you've been driven out of your home in search of work.

In cities, bread lines wrap around the block. In places such as California and Florida, workers called migrants follow the harvests. They constantly search for work picking crops.

That is your life now—on the move. You live day-to-day, just hoping you'll be able to eat. You do backbreaking work for little pay, without much hope of a better future.

You're a dusty face in the crowd. Where will your next job come from? What about your next meal? Step back in time and experience the life of a migrant worker during the Great Depression.

- To be a white child traveling with your family from Oklahoma to California, turn to page 11.

- To struggle as a Black migrant worker in the Southeast, turn to page 45.

- To look for work as a Mexican-American in southern California, turn to page 69.

CHAPTER 2

FLEEING THE DUST BOWL

The constant bumping and shaking of your wagon almost lulls you to sleep. You sit in the rear of the wagon, your feet hanging off the back. Your worn boots dangle above the two dirt ruts that serve as a road.

"You all right back there?" calls your mom. She's sitting up front with your dad as he guides the family's pack horse along the road. The three of you take turns driving, but your dad does most of it.

Turn the page.

You begged your dad to get an automobile for the trip. But even if he could afford a car, there was no way he could pay for the gas to drive it to California. You tell yourself that traveling like people did in the Old West is exciting.

Migrant workers following the wheat harvest

"I'm good," you call back, even though you don't really feel that way. Your life has been turned upside down. You've left behind everyone you know to head west into an uncertain future.

No, you don't feel good at all. But your parents have enough to worry about. Your baby brother, Edward, has been sick with a cough for weeks. Both he and your mom cry at night. You can see the stress and sense of helplessness on your dad's face. You've made it your job not to add to their burden.

You gaze to the southeast—back in the direction of home. At least that used to be home. An ominous dark cloud hangs over the landscape in the distance. It's a dust storm—a sight that has become all too familiar in the past few years. The storms have displaced many farm families, most of them white like yours.

Turn the page.

You shake your head. Everything was good. Your family had a small homestead in Oklahoma. Your dad farmed the land—with your help when you weren't busy with school. You had friends, a happy life, and a future.

When the economy collapsed in 1929, it felt like a distant problem. Then the next year, the dust storms began. As winds howled, the topsoil that farmers depended on whipped up in huge, rolling clouds. With the topsoil stripped and drought leaving everything dry, your crops failed two years in a row.

By the spring of 1932, your family had no choice. You packed up your few belongings and headed west to California.

"There will be work there," your father explained. "The land there is still good. We'll make it work."

After two days on the road, you reach Oklahoma City. Your dad sells your horse and wagon and buys train tickets. "On to California," he says, forcing a smile.

The train carries you west, across rolling plains and into the desert. You watch out the window as the train winds through mountain passes. Finally, you reach California. As promised, the land is green, and farms are plentiful. But so are workers. Migrants like you line up for jobs, eager to do backbreaking work for little pay.

Your family makes a home in a tiny wooden shack, surrounded by other migrant workers. You find an old wood stove with a stovepipe discarded in a pile of trash nearby and set it up to provide heat on cool nights.

Turn the page.

After a few days, your father finds a job on a nearby farm. He plows, plants, bales hay, and does any other jobs that are needed.

The job is a stroke of luck. Most migrants work for large single-crop farms, traveling from place to place. Finding steady employment on a smaller family farm is unusual. But the pay is barely enough to feed the family.

"We need more income," your father says one night with a sigh.

Edward starts to cry. Your mother looks exhausted. Should you volunteer to work? Or should you take care of the baby so your mother can join your father?

- To take care of Edward while your parents work, go to the next page.
- To join your father working in the fields, turn to page 20.

You pick up your brother and bounce him gently until he stops crying. "Mom, Dad," you begin. "I can take care of Edward during the day, if that would help."

Your mother reluctantly agrees. "I hate to leave him, but I don't think you're old enough for field work yet," she says. You can see by the lines on her face that she is torn by the decision. None of her choices have been easy lately. All she can do is pick the lesser of two evils, and that's to leave you with the baby.

The next day, she's out in search of work. It's just you and Edward in your little shack. That afternoon, while he is napping, you step outside.

A little town has sprung up here. It's filled with shacks like yours. People mill up and down the streets. They're all "Okies" like you.

Turn the page.

The name started because so many migrants came from Oklahoma. But now, it just refers to anyone who has come here in search of work.

"Hey kid," a voice calls out. A man dressed in a plaid shirt and overalls waves from across the dirt road that runs through the shantytown. "Got a minute?"

"How can I help you?" you ask.

The man waves you over. A pile of logs sits alongside his shack.

A shantytown in 1932

"Name's Hank. Hurt my back at work yesterday, but I need this wood split for my stove. I don't have any spare money to pay you, but I have this." He shows you a small burlap sack. "It's a pound of sugar. I took it in trade last week, but I have no use for it. What do you say?"

You glance over your shoulder. Edward should be sound asleep for at least another hour. And the wood pile isn't that big. Your shelves are pretty bare. That sugar could have some real value to your family. Can you trust that your brother won't need you for a little while?

• To take the job, turn to page 22.
• To decline, turn to page 25.

"I can work too," you say.

Your mother shakes her head. "No, you're too young. You don't belong out in the fields."

You insist. "I'm strong and healthy. And staying here all day does me no good. Let me work."

Migrant workers picking lettuce

It takes time, but your father agrees, and you eventually wear down your mother. The next morning, you head out with your father.

"Morning," he calls out to his supervisor, Chuck, as you arrive on the farm. He introduces you and asks if you can help with the work.

Chuck looks you up and down and shrugs. "Why not," he mumbles. "A dollar for the day. We'll see how it works out."

It's a small sum for a day's work. But you just want to prove your value.

Workers gather into two groups. One is going to cut and bale hay. Your dad is in that group. A second group is going out to harvest grapes. Which group should you join?

• To join your dad to bale hay, turn to page 27.
• To pick grapes instead, turn to page 39.

After a moment of hesitation, you agree. "Sure, mister. Happy to help."

Hank sets you up with a large axe. It's heavy, and it takes you a few tries to get the hang of it, but soon you're splitting logs in two. It's tiring work, and it takes you almost an hour to finish. But Hank rewards you with the bag of sugar.

"Thanks," you tell him, rushing back across the street. The weight of it in your hand feels good. You beam with the knowledge that you've managed to help out a little more.

Edward is still asleep as you enter your shack. You let out a deep breath. If he had been awake and crying, you would have felt awful.

When the baby wakes up, you walk down to a small fruit stand set up outside of town. Your mother left you a dime to pick up some produce.

The stand has fresh fruit, including apples and berries. But you spend the money on a few potatoes. They'll go a lot farther toward feeding everyone tonight. That evening, your parents are exhausted. But they're excited to hear about your small job and grateful for your addition to the family's small pantry.

A fruit stand during the Great Depression

Turn the page.

"What about the baby?" your mother asks. You go silent for a moment, realizing that they'll be mad if you admit to leaving Edward alone.

"He slept through it all," you answer. Your parents assume that you meant that he was with you, and you don't correct them. You realize that if you want to make extra cash again, you're going to need to have the baby with you from now on.

You spend the night thinking about how you might make more money. What if you set up your own produce stand? Maybe you could turn a profit by selling fruit and vegetables. It would take work and some resources to get started, though. Maybe it would be better just to go into town searching for odd jobs.

• To start a produce stand, turn to page 34.
• To look for odd jobs, turn to page 37.

"Sorry mister," you answer. "My baby brother is sleeping. I have to keep an eye on him."

Hank shrugs. He seems surprised that anyone would turn down even a small job. But you know that watching your brother is your job right now. If both of your parents can work, you'll have a chance to keep the family fed during these hard times.

You spend your days with Edward. Your dad works long hours in the fields, while your mother takes any odd jobs she can find. You are truly living day-to-day. There's not always enough food. You always take small portions and claim that you're not hungry—even when your stomach is rumbling. You know your dad would starve himself to keep you fed, but he needs his strength to work.

Turn the page.

With fall comes the harvest season, meaning even longer hours for your parents. The nights get cooler in your little home. One day, while your parents are gone, Edward's cough grows alarmingly bad. As the hours pass, it gets worse and worse. The little boy is struggling to breathe. He looks pale and glassy-eyed.

You check the coffee can where your parents keep what little cash you have. There's only five dollars inside. Not nearly enough for a doctor. What can you do?

- To go to a doctor anyway, turn to page 29.
- To care for Edward at home, turn to page 32.

You climb onto a wagon and sit next to your dad. In the field, you and six other workers use large blades called scythes to cut bundles of hay. It's hard work. You wear an old pair of your dad's work gloves, but your hands still blister from the work.

From there, you haul the hay to a wagon, where it is taken to a large baling machine. Chuck looks on as you help load hay into the baler. The machine squeezes the hay into tight, square bales.

Your first few attempts don't go well. You don't get enough hay into the machine, so the bales are loose. Chuck just shakes his head.

"Keep at it," says your dad, as he pulls a bale out of the machine and loads it onto the trailer. You get back to work, stuffing more hay into the machine. "Okay, go," you say.

Turn the page.

But as you step back, you can already tell that once again it won't be good enough. Quickly, you grab an armful of hay. You could stuff some more in before it's too late. You don't want to give Chuck another reason not to bring you back tomorrow. But is it worth the risk? The machine is already starting. If you're not quick enough, you could get injured.

- To quickly stuff more hay in, turn to page 41.
- To wait, turn to page 42.

Your brother is desperately ill. You have to do something. You scoop out the five dollar bill, wrap Edward in a warm blanket, and head out.

Your shantytown sits on the outskirts of town. It's a twenty-minute walk to the closest doctor's office. A bell rings as you walk inside.

"Hello. Can I help you?" asks a slim, dark-haired woman. A name tag identifies her as Maria.

"My brother is sick," you explain.

"Do you have an appointment?" she asks in a sharp tone. You shake your head. Edward lets out a cough and a weak cry.

Maria sighs, "I'm sorry. But Dr. Alvarez is—"

"Send them back," booms a voice from the back room. A gray-haired man peeks out of the doorway. "Come, come," he says.

Turn the page.

Dr. Alvarez gives you a smile as he looks over Edward. He pulls a small bottle off of a shelf. "Here, take this. Give your brother two doses a day until it's gone."

"Thank you doctor," you say. You pull the wrinkled five-dollar bill from your pocket and hand it to the doctor. "I know it's not enough, but it's all we have."

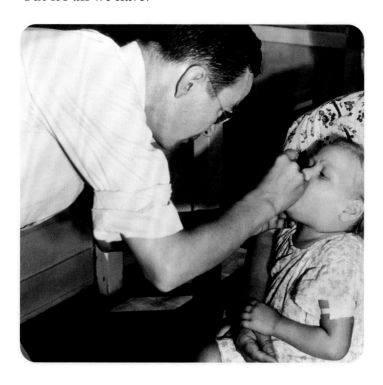

The doctor takes the bill. He reaches into his pocket, then hands it back to you. Stunned, you look down. Along with your five dollars, he's given you a crisp twenty-dollar bill. It's more money than you've ever held at one time.

Dr. Alvarez claps you on the back. "Now, get Edward home. Keep him warm, and give him lots of water. If that cough doesn't clear up in a few days, come back and see me."

As you walk out of the office, you can't stop thinking of the doctor's kindness. Times are tough. But people are still good. For the first time, you really start to believe that you and your family will make it through this troubling time.

THE END

To follow another path, turn to page 9.
To learn more about surviving the Great Depression, turn to page 99.

You feel helpless. Edward is getting sicker by the hour, and there's nothing you can do. He's so weak, he barely even cries anymore. You wrap him in blankets. You try to get him to drink water. But he just spits everything back up.

Your mom comes home that evening. She's exhausted from working all day, but she stays up with Edward all night. In the morning, she heads into town to see a doctor. You wait back in your little shack.

It's the last time you see your brother. The illness is too much for his weak little body, and he doesn't recover. Your life is forever changed. You so badly wish that you hadn't been too worried about money to take him to the doctor sooner. You're never able to forgive yourself.

In time, the Great Depression passes. Your father finds steady work. Your mother never fully recovers from the pain of losing a child. But she survives. And you set out to begin a life of your own. But you know there will always be a hole in your heart. You'll never be able to put the loss of your brother and the dark days of the Great Depression behind you.

THE END

To follow another path, turn to page 9.
To learn more about surviving the Great Depression, turn to page 99.

The more you think about it, the more excited you are about starting your own fruit stand. The next day, you get started. You grab a few dollars from the coffee can and head out. With Edward in his old stroller, you walk from farm to farm. You buy small amounts of carrots, lettuce, apples, grapes, and berries. You find a spot along the road into town. You stack some cinder blocks up and lay an old board across it.

The plan is a disaster. You sell almost nothing. At the end of the day, you're left with a pile of produce. "Oh, well," you mutter. "At least we can still eat all of this. It won't go to waste."

When you get home, a new idea comes to you. You've got sugar and berries, along with flour, a few eggs, and other ingredients. You fire up the old wood stove and get baking. The next day, you set up shop again—this time with freshly baked muffins.

An old wood-burning stove

This time, your business venture is a hit. Workers stop by on their way to the fields. In less than an hour, you sell each of the two dozen muffins you made. You take the money and use it to buy more ingredients. Day by day, your business grows. You make more—and sell more.

Turn the page.

Your dad shakes his head as he looks at the money you're earning. "You're making more than me some days," he says. "I think you've found your calling."

He's right. Over the next few years, you continue your stand. Your mom stops working and helps out. She runs a second stand on the other side of town. You build a loyal customer base. Soon, your family can afford a proper little house in town.

The Great Depression is a difficult time. But you got lucky. You found a way to help your family. You're going to survive the tough times. And who knows? Maybe one day, you can open your own store and start a career as a baker.

THE END

To follow another path, turn to page 9.
To learn more about surviving the Great Depression, turn to page 99.

Starting your own business feels like such a big task. What if you used the family's precious money and lost it all? You'd never forgive yourself.

"No," you tell Edward the next morning. "It's too risky." The baby smiles and laughs as he plays with a rubber ball.

You load Edward into a stroller and head into town. You walk up and down the streets. You knock on doors. You talk to store owners.

"Have you got any work?" you ask. The answer is almost always, "No."

Sometimes, people will press a few cents into your palm. You hate taking charity. But you never turn it down. Each day, you head back into town. Some days, you earn a few nickels. One day, you make a whole dollar by painting a woman's house.

Turn the page.

But it's only a drop in the bucket. Your family is barely getting by. It's only a matter of time before you'll need to work in the fields too.

You try to stay optimistic. But times are tough. You're living day-to-day, and it doesn't look like that will change anytime soon. All you can do is your best. Your dad says the bad times will pass. You have to believe him. It's all that gets you through the day sometimes.

THE END

To follow another path, turn to page 9.
To learn more about surviving the Great Depression, turn to page 99.

You join the grape-picking crew. The work isn't quite as backbreaking as baling hay. Since you're young and inexperienced, it just makes more sense.

You spend the day in the hot sun, carefully plucking ripe bunches of grapes from vines that line the field. Your arms and shoulders ache from the constant effort. No matter how hard you try, you seem to be slower and less productive than the other workers.

Migrant workers picking grapes

Turn the page.

It's your first day, and you're sure you can get better. But Chuck decides that he'd rather hire more experienced workers. The next day, you're back at home with Edward and your mother.

Over the next few years, the family moves from place to place. You join your dad in the fields whenever you can. But it's a constant search for work.

Someday, all of this will end. You dream of returning to Oklahoma to live on a farm of your own. But right now, those dreams seem very far away.

THE END

To follow another path, turn to page 9.
To learn more about surviving the Great Depression, turn to page 99.

You have time. You quickly dart forward, reaching out to put more hay in before the baler compresses the bale. But as you move, you stumble. Your hand reaches out to catch your fall—and it slips right beneath one of the metal plates that creates the square bale.

It's a disaster. Before anyone can stop it, the baler does its thing. The bones in your hand crunch and snap as you scream in pain. Chuck runs over and shuts down the machine. But the damage is done. You black out from the pain.

Your hand is injured beyond repair. You'll never be able to use it again. You wanted to help your parents make it through these difficult times. You failed. And you'll be paying for that for the rest of your life.

THE END

To follow another path, turn to page 9.
To learn more about surviving the Great Depression, turn to page 99.

You start to move toward the baler but quickly stop yourself. That would be a terrible idea. The big machine would crush your hand if it got stuck. Better to wait.

On the next try, you get it right. The bale comes out perfectly. "Good job," Chuck says with a nod. You get better and faster as the day goes on. It was a rough start, but you finished strong and proved that you can do the work.

An antique baler

"Come on back tomorrow," Chuck tells you at the end of the day. "You're a good worker. I'll give you a dollar and a half a day. It's fair pay, in these times."

You smile and nod. You know that it's not very good pay at all. But there are far more workers than there are jobs out here. You have to take whatever you can get. You'll do all you can to help your family get through these times. Maybe you can help build a better future for little Edward.

THE END

To follow another path, turn to page 9.
To learn more about surviving the Great Depression, turn to page 99.

CHAPTER 3

OUT OF THE CITY

A warm breeze blows across your face as you walk down a dusty country road. You look around you. It feels like another planet. You've spent your life in the heart of Atlanta, surrounded by people, buildings, and automobiles. Out here, the open spaces seem like something out of a movie.

"Keep up," Charlie says, looking over his shoulder.

Turn the page.

You pick up the pace to catch up to your friend. The two of you make a bit of an odd pair. You're both young men from the city. But Charlie is white, and you're Black. In a time—and a place—where laws separate the races in many parts of society, the two of you are a rarity.

But no matter your color, you face the same financial struggle right now. The factory that you both worked in shut down. After weeks looking for work in the city, you finally had no choice. You were forced to either leave to find farmwork in the country or starve.

You became friends on the factory floor. Now, you're traveling companions.

Fields of cotton stretch as far as the eye can see. A sign reads "HIRING" along a lane toward one of the big farms. It's harvest time, and farmers are looking for help picking their cotton crop.

"What do you think?" Charlie asks. "I know you said that you didn't want to pick cotton, but work is work."

The idea of working in a cotton field fills you with dread. Your great-grandparents had been enslaved on cotton farms. Your ancestors might have worked these very fields. It makes you sick to think of what they went through.

"I don't know, Charlie," you reply. "I thought we were headed to Florida. We said we were going to go pick fruit, not cotton."

Charlie shrugs. He doesn't understand why you're so reluctant to work on a cotton farm. "So maybe we make a stop along the way. There's work here." Charlie pats the backpack he's wearing. "We've only got so much food and even less money. Can we afford to pass up work?"

Turn the page.

Charlie can't possibly understand your turmoil. You know the color of your skin doesn't matter to him. But it frustrates you that he doesn't seem to notice how much harder the world is for a person with dark skin.

"Well?" Charlie asks. He brushes his dark curly hair from his eyes. "I say let's do it. We need every dollar we can earn. And farmers like this probably feed their workers a proper meal."

He's got a point. Still, you're not sure. You take a moment before you tell him what you think.

• To look for work here, go to the next page.
• To continue south to Florida, turn to page 51.

You haven't worked in more than a month. You don't like it, but you have to take any job you can get. "Okay, let's check it out," you say.

It's a large family-run farm. The owners have a few hired men who handle most of the work. But it's harvest time, and they need extra hands. They offer you and Charlie jobs. You'll be paid based on how much you pick—probably a few dollars a day.

A sign advertises for migrant workers.

Turn the page.

The first day is slow. You don't make much money. But you soon get the hang of it. By the second day, you're producing a lot more.

Day three is scorching hot. The sun beats down on you all day, and there's no shade in the cotton fields. The farmers keep a cooler of water at one end of the field. But by midafternoon, you're on the opposite side. As you pick, you find yourself feeling faint. You notice that you're not sweating.

"You don't look good," Charlie yells from a few rows down. "Do you need a break?"

Maybe you should go get some water. But that's going to take time—time that you're not picking and earning.

• To go get water, turn to page 57.
• To keep working, turn to page 63.

"Let's stick to the plan, Charlie," you reply. "We can be in Florida in a few days. Think about it. We can be out in a beautiful orchard, picking fruit. We'll have the shade of the trees and the bright blue Florida sky. Doesn't that sound better than sweating in a sunbaked cotton field?"

Charlie shrugs, but he doesn't argue. The two of you continue south. Along the way, you hitch a ride in the back of a rusty truck. Within two days, you're in the heart of Florida's citrus country. You find a large orchard that is hiring migrant workers to pick oranges.

At dawn, a dozen men and women wait at the gate. A middle-aged white man steps out. "Good morning, everyone," he says. "I'm Peter. We're hiring eight workers today." You stand tall, trying to look strong and able. The man points out his choices one by one. You're in luck—both you and Charlie are among his selections.

Turn the page.

"Two dollars for the day," Peter tells Charlie as he walks through the gate. Charlie nods in agreement. As you follow, Peter gives you a hard look. "A dollar-fifty for the day," he says.

You stop. Did you hear him right? "What? You said two dollars."

Peter leans in. He's missing one of his front teeth, and his breath smells like stale coffee. "That's more than fair for you," he says. You know he's referring to your skin color. "If you don't want it, I can find someone else."

Rage swells up in your gut. You feel insulted and belittled. Why should you take less money just because of the color of your skin? Should you speak up for yourself? Or should you take what you can get? Racism is thick here. Standing up for yourself could get you beaten or killed

• To take the job, go to the next page.
• To demand equal pay, turn to page 55.

You know your worth, but you need whatever money you can make. "Yes sir," you answer.

Peter pats you on the shoulder. "Now, that's a good lad," he says. "Let's get to work."

It's a long day of picking oranges. You fill basket after basket. When you get tired, you just keep going. Peter is always watching you. You feel like you're always on trial.

Migrant workers in a peach orchard

Turn the page.

The pay may be lacking, but the food here is good. Lunch includes roasted chicken, potatoes, green beans, and even a chocolate cake. It's the best meal you've eaten in months.

At the end of the day, Peter pulls you and Charlie aside. "You're good workers. Are you interested in staying? We have a few bunks set up in the barn. They're yours if you want them."

It's what you wanted—steady work. But can you stay here, working for less money because you're Black? Charlie quickly accepts the offer. It's not so easy for you, however. There will be other jobs out there. Maybe jobs where you're treated as an equal. That's what you really want. But you're unsure if there's any opportunity out there that's better than this.

• To decline the offer, turn to page 59.
• To accept, turn to page 61.

You stand tall and look Peter in the eye. "I can do the work as well as any man, no matter his skin color," you say. "If you're paying the others two dollars, then do the same for me."

A broad smile stretches across the man's face. For a moment, you believe you've convinced him.

Then he laughs. "Get off my farm," he demands, suddenly turning very serious. "You," he shouts, pointing to one of the migrants who hadn't been chosen. "Come. This one doesn't want to work."

As the gate closes, you stand outside. You have nowhere to go. Nothing to do. You wait nearby for your friend. It's a long day, and you're low on food. That evening, when Charlie finishes his work, you greet him.

"Should we keep moving?" you ask. "I'm sure we can find another orchard."

Turn the page.

Charlie shakes his head. "I'm sorry. But they really like me here. Peter said I'd get three dollars if I come back. I can't leave this behind. Please understand."

• Turn to page 59.

"I think I'm dehydrated," you call back. Charlie walks you to the water cooler. A close look at your friend tells you that he's on the verge of dehydration too. The two of you sit in the shade of a tree and drink the cool water.

After a few minutes, Charlie heads back to the fields, while you continue to rest. You know every minute you spend here is costing you money. But your body is telling you that all is not well.

The next day, you try again. But for whatever reason, the heat just seems to affect you more than it does Charlie and the other workers. You end each day feeling completely drained. You're not sure how long your body will hold up.

After a lot of careful thinking, you realize that this isn't the job for you. "I think I need to move on," you tell Charlie.

Turn the page.

He looks torn. "They've offered me a job here full-time," Charlie says. "One of the other men is leaving after the harvest. I have to take it."

You don't blame him. He's thriving out here, while you're struggling.

You and Charlie left Atlanta as traveling companions. You never agreed to stay together forever. You just hoped that if you had to live on the road, it could be with a friend. But there's no place for you here. It's time to move on.

"Good luck to you, my friend," Charlie says, shaking your hand.

"You too," you say. "Here's hoping we meet again."

With that, you're back on the road—this time alone. You pick up a few jobs as you travel. But it's a life on the road. You're lonely and constantly worried about where you'll sleep and what you'll eat.

One day, as you make your way farther south toward the fruit orchards, you come across a small farm. An older Black man named Cassius greets you.

Turn the page.

"Welcome," he says. Cassius owns and runs the small peanut farm by himself. But his health is declining.

"I can't pay you much," he says. "But I can offer room, board, and what little money I can spare."

This clearly isn't much of an answer to your money problems. But the chance to stay in one place for a while is appealing. Plus, Cassius would be daily company. What should you do?

- To move on, turn to page 64.
- To join Cassius, turn to page 66.

This is what you wanted when you left Atlanta—steady work, food, and a place to stay. You resent the situation you're in, but you accept the offer. Doing the same job for less pay is an insult. But this is the Deep South in the 1930s. Racism runs rampant. You don't see any better option for yourself right now.

Migrant workers weighing cotton

Turn the page.

As hired men, you and Charlie do all sorts of work around the farm. You pick fruit, prune trees, build and mend fences, dig trenches, and fix whatever needs fixing. The work is hard, but you take pride in a job well done.

Months pass—then years. You save most of what you earn. And by the late 1930s, when the Great Depression is coming to an end, you have enough money saved to follow a new dream. You buy a small farm of your own. The world is changing all around you, and you're ready to change with it. It's time to start the next chapter of your life.

THE END

To follow another path, turn to page 9.
To learn more about surviving the Great Depression, turn to page 99.

You shake your head. "I'm fine," you call back.

You get back to work. But as time passes, you feel worse and worse. Late in the afternoon, a sudden wave of nausea hits you. Darkness creeps in around the edges of your eyes. You faint before you realize what's happening. When you regain consciousness, you're lying on the ground with Charlie at your side.

"Help!" Charlie cries out. "Someone get water! I think he's got heat stroke!"

The other workers try to help you. But it's too late. Your body is dehydrated and overheated. Your organs are shutting down. Farmwork is hard, and your body wasn't up to it. You pushed yourself too far, and the price is your life.

THE END

To follow another path, turn to page 9.
To learn more about surviving the Great Depression,
turn to page 99.

You thank Cassius for the offer. "I'm afraid I'm broke," you explain. "I need to find a job where I can earn more money." The old man wishes you well.

Now, you're back on the road. It's a hard life. You move from job to job. Sometimes, you go days at a time with almost nothing to eat.

Racism runs deep in this part of the country. You face hatred and injustice at every turn. People call you offensive names. You're forced to accept less pay than white workers. Sometimes, you're not allowed to sleep in buildings with your white coworkers. You share the barn with the animals.

Such poor treatment wears you down. All you can do is keep your head high and work as hard as you can every chance you get. You travel all along the panhandle of Florida and up and down the Gulf Coast.

Workers hoeing cotton fields

Being on the move is a difficult life, but it's the best you can do. Maybe someday, things will get better. Because you're not sure how much longer you can keep going this way.

THE END

To follow another path, turn to page 9.
To learn more about surviving the Great Depression, turn to page 99.

Sure, the pay won't be good, but you're glad for a little stability and some company.

"That sounds good to me," you reply.

Over the next few months, Cassius teaches you the ins and outs of peanut farming. The pay is almost nothing—less than a dollar a day. But you have a bed, food, and good company. And you feel like you belong.

The next spring, Cassius grows ill. A doctor comes to visit, and the news is grim. "I'm afraid he doesn't have much time," the doctor explains.

You feel terrible for Cassius. He's a kind man, and he's become like family. But you also wonder what it means for you. Will you be back on the road again? The idea fills you with dread.

That night, Cassius calls you into his bedroom. He looks so weak. Cassius takes you by the hand.

"You've been a wonderful worker," he starts. "I have no children of my own. I would like to leave you the farm when I pass. You can make a living here. Maybe start a family. What do you say?"

You can barely get out a "Yes," as the tears well up in your eyes. Somehow, in all the pain and desperation of the Great Depression, you've managed to find a future here. That stroke of luck will help you through the loss of your friend.

THE END

To follow another path, turn to page 9.
To learn more about surviving the Great Depression,
turn to page 99.

CHAPTER 4

CHANGING TIMES

The old dusty road is familiar. You've been here before. Since you were fourteen years old, you've made this yearly trek with the men in your family. It's harvest season in the American Southwest, and you follow the crops.

"Me pregunto si ha sido un buen año," Pablo asks, wondering in Spanish if it's been a good year for the crops. You all know some English, but when you're together, you speak in your native language. You're American by birth—a U.S. citizen. But most of your family members were born in Mexico. You work as migrants.

Turn the page.

Your father, brothers, uncles, and cousins trace a familiar path each year. The farmers you work for know you, from Baja all the way up to central California. For six years, you've come here, to this avocado farm in southern California. You know exactly when crops will be ready, and farmers will need your help. But as you walk up to the familiar farm, you see something new. There are others here. Men and women line up, ready and eager to work.

Your father shakes his head. "What is this?"

You know. The Great Depression has hit Mexico too. The work you've always depended on is now in high demand.

A farmhand stands before the gathered crowd. You recognize Hank's broad shoulders and long, scruffy beard. You catch his eye and nod. He waves you over.

Turn the page.

Harvesting avocados

"I was wondering if we'd see you," he says in a low voice. "It's been a strange year. So many people are out of work. They're lining up for the chance to work. I've already hired most of my crew. I've got a spot for you if you want it, but just one. And the pay is a bit lower than you're used to. I can only offer half of what you got last year."

The news shocks you. But it probably shouldn't. One look around you tells you why. If you turn down the offer, there are a dozen others who will gladly take it.

"Give me a minute," you answer. Hank nods.

You walk back to where your father and the rest of your family wait. You give them the bad news. "They only have work for one," you report. "And the pay is not good."

Your father closes his eyes and shakes his head. "What do you think?" he asks.

You could take the job and catch up with your family farther north. Or you could stick together, in hopes of finding a place with work for all of you. You don't love either choice, but you have to decide.

• To take the job, turn to page 74.

• To move on with your family, turn to page 76.

You're here to work, even if that means it's just you. Separating from the others is only temporary. You can reconnect later. And if not, you'll all return home to Mexico after the harvest season. You shake hands, give hugs, and bid your family farewell. It's time to harvest.

The hot sun beats down as you move from tree to tree. Many of the other workers are slow. They've never done this before. You get frustrated with their pace, but you keep going.

After a hard day's work, Hank hands out your pay—just a couple of dollars. "Is this for real, Hank?" you ask, looking at the money. "We got twice this just last year."

Hank just shakes his head. "I'm so sorry," he tells you. "But times are tight. There are 100 other people who would take the job for even less money."

"But you know me," you tell him. "You know my family. We've worked here for years. I'm a better worker than those other people, and I can barely live on these wages."

Your mind is racing. What can you do about it?

• To demand more money, turn to page 80.
• To stay quiet, turn to page 82.

You need a job. But the idea of splitting up with your family is too much. They are all you have. Nothing is more important.

"I'm sorry," you tell Hank. "I have to stay with my family."

Hank nods. "I understand. Everything is crazy right now. So many people are desperate for work. Let's just hope things get back to normal soon. Come back next year. You'll always have a place here if we have the openings."

You wish Hank well and continue on your way. Every year is a constant struggle for survival. But it's worse than usual. Everywhere you go, workers are lined up, eager to take the work that was once yours. You're barely earning enough to survive.

Turn the page.

Unemployed workers waiting in line for a job

But one day, things get even worse. You and your family are with a larger group of Mexican migrants camping outside a small farming community. A local sheriff and deputies suddenly surround you.

"It's a raid!" shouts Javier, your cousin.

"Don't resist!" says a voice over a bullhorn. "If you are in this country illegally, you will be transported back to Mexico."

You've heard of deportation raids. But you never imagined it would happen to you. You know you're an American citizen, but will these men believe you?

And what about your family members who aren't? They've been working this land for years. How can the authorities do this to the people who have been growing their food for so long?

"We should run," Javier says. He's sweating. His eyes dart back and forth, looking for an escape.

You take a quick scan. The sheriff and his deputies have positioned themselves on all sides of the camp. But there aren't enough of them. If enough people run, some of you are bound to get away.

Should you run? Or is it too risky?

• To run, turn to page 93.
• To stay put, turn to page 95.

"Hank, it's just not enough. You need to pay me more, or I'll find something else. I know there are others who will take this job. But I watched some of the new people today. I'm worth more than they are."

It's a bold stand to take. At first, you think Hank might tell you to go ahead and leave. But then his expression softens.

"Look," he says. "I could use another crew supervisor. You're right—a lot of these people have never done this before. They don't have your knowledge or your work ethic. If you want to lead a crew for me tomorrow, I can double this."

You quickly agree. With that, you're in charge of half a dozen newcomers. Over the next week, you teach your workers and make sure everyone stays on track. The pay is better, and you feel that you've earned every cent.

Once the avocado harvest is over, it's time to move on. "Good luck," Hank tells you. "I have a friend about thirty miles south of here. They're just getting started on their harvest. I know he'll need supervisors as well. I can give you a reference if you want. He'll pay you well."

Your whole goal is to earn as much money during harvest as you can. But your family is north. If you head south, you may not see them again for months. Is it worth it?

• To go north in search of your family, turn to page 83.
• To go south and take the job, turn to page 96.

Hank just shrugs. You think about asking for more money, but it's pointless. There are so many workers competing for jobs now that they'll just hire the next one. There was a time before the Great Depression where you could afford to take a stand. But now you have to take what you can get.

You spend a week on the job, picking avocados in the hot California sun. It is exhausting, back-breaking work, but you're used to it. Your hands get calloused. Your body grows accustomed to the heat and sun.

When the harvest is done, you move on. You head north, in search of the next job. But what you really hope to find is your family. You pray that they've found work as well. You hope everyone is healthy and that they've been able to stick together.

As you travel north, you work odd jobs, picking berries, tomatoes, peppers, and more. Like you, many other longtime Mexican and Mexican-American workers are struggling. Wages are low. Competition is high. And they are facing more and more hatred and violence from white workers.

A migrant worker picking melons

Turn the page.

Along the way, you enter a small town. A large group of white men on horseback blocks your way. "You're not welcome here," calls out a large, broad-shouldered man. "Americans only."

"I'm a citizen," you call back in English. "I was born here."

The man spits and glares at you. "Whites only," he specifies. Apparently, he's so racist he doesn't think darker-skinned people count as Americans.

Rage swells up inside you. How dare they question your right to be here? Are they serious enough to try to stop you? You consider walking right past them and into town. But you don't want any trouble from these racist men.

• To turn around, go to the next page.
• To ignore them and march into town, turn to page 87.

You turn around. You don't need to go through this town. There's no reason to pick a fight here. The wise move is to go around.

As you move north to your next destination, you can only shake your head. People will always look for someone to blame for their troubles. It's not your fault. You're just looking to make a living, like anyone else. But some white people are going to blame you for taking jobs that they want anyway. You can't let it bother you.

A few days later, you manage to meet back up with your family. They've been working job-by-job, just like you.

"Have you heard?" your father asks you. "Mexico is trying to lure Mexican migrants and their American-born children back to their country. They are offering land if we'll return to Mexico."

Turn the page.

You are shocked. "Really?" The anti-Mexican stance that many white people have during this crisis has left you feeling uneasy about life here. If it's true, the promise of your own land is appealing. But your family has lived the life of migrant workers for longer than you've been alive. It's all you know.

Of course, that means you know how farms operate. The difference is migrant workers get paid during the good years and the bad years. If it's your own farm, crop failure will affect you much more. Are you really ready for the responsibility of managing your own land?

You grow very quiet as you walk with your relatives. Your mind races. What should you do?

- To return to Mexico in hopes of getting your own land, turn to page 89.

- To continue as a migrant worker, turn to page 91.

Your anger and pride get the better of you. "Get out of my way," you tell them as you continue along the road. "I have every right to be here."

You square your shoulders, tighten your jaw, and put on a look of confidence as you march forward. The dirt crunches under your boots as you ignore the men. It's a show of strength and confidence that you hope—and believe—will force them to back down. They're bluffing, and you're calling their bluff.

It is a terrible decision. The hard times have made people desperate. They're looking for someone to blame. And many white people blame people of Mexican descent. They believe you are taking their jobs. They have wrongly convinced themselves that you are the root of all the problems that plague them.

Turn the page.

You made a gamble that these men were all talk and no action. You were wrong. As you walk forward, they surround you. They're armed, angry, and not willing to listen to reason. That's a bad combination.

As the mob attacks, you realize your mistake. You won't be reconnecting with your family. Hunger and unemployment made some people desperate and angry. And today, you're the one they blame for all their troubles.

The men beat you until the world fades away. You knew that the life of a migrant worker was dangerous. But you never really believed it would cost you your life.

THE END

To follow another path, turn to page 9.
To learn more about surviving the Great Depression, turn to page 99.

Land of your own—you can't get the idea out of your mind. You've never owned land. Your father has never owned land. His father has never owned land.

You know what you want to do. "I'm going back to Mexico," you tell your father later that day. You expect him to be disappointed that you're leaving. But a big smile spreads across his face. "Good," he says, nodding.

You speak to a few others about the idea, but no one else is willing to leave in the middle of harvest season.

You hit the road alone. This time, you go south. Along the way, you meet others chasing the same dream. They confirm the rumor that Mexico wants you back. They are enticing Mexican-Americans to return to Mexico by offering up land.

Turn the page.

A field of agave plants, often grown in Mexico

As you cross the border into Mexico, you are filled with hope. A new life awaits you. You know it won't be easy. But your days as a migrant worker are over. The next time you harvest a crop, it will be your own.

THE END

To follow another path, turn to page 9.
To learn more about surviving the Great Depression, turn to page 99.

Owning land sounds great at first. But the more you think about it, the less sure you are that you can do it. You've always been a migrant worker. It's a hard life, but it's the life you know. If you own your own farm, you must become a businessperson as well. You could make more money. But you'll also take more risks—a few bad harvests could ruin you.

You decide to continue moving from job to job. It's long hours and backbreaking work for little pay. But you keep moving. You keep scraping by.

The Great Depression is filled with dark days. You face hatred and racism. You survive on little pay, often going hungry for days at a time. But the darkness passes. By the end of the 1930s, things are improving.

Turn the page.

When the United States enters World War II (1939–1945) in 1941, there is plenty of work and better pay. Still, racism is ever-present in the United States. You always wonder if you made the right choice. What might life have been like if you'd gone back to Mexico for good? You'll never know for sure.

THE END

To follow another path, turn to page 9.
To learn more about surviving the Great Depression, turn to page 99.

"Let's go," you whisper to Javier. You'd like to tell the rest of your family, but there's no time.

"There," Javier says, pointing to a spot where you might slip away. "Follow me."

You move quickly, darting out of the camp. One of the deputies notices you and shouts "Freeze!" But he doesn't make a move to stop you. Together, you and Javier slip out of the camp and keep running until you find the cover of some trees.

Your heart is thumping as you take cover and look back. No one followed you.

"Why didn't they chase us?" Javier asks between deep breaths.

"I guess they got what they wanted," you reply. "They didn't care about us because there are dozens of people back there who didn't run."

Turn the page.

You watch from your hiding spot. In horror, you see the rest of the people in the camp being loaded into trucks. Deportation raids have become more and more common during the Great Depression. And you just escaped one.

But now, it's just you and Javier, trying to find work together in a hostile land. Most white people wrongly blame you for their suffering. They see you as a foreigner here to take their jobs.

Life will be even more difficult from now on. But you keep moving, from farm to farm. You won't thrive. But you'll survive. Maybe that's all anyone can ask for these days. You only hope to have some money to bring home to your family when the harvest season is over.

THE END

To follow another path, turn to page 9.
To learn more about surviving the Great Depression, turn to page 99.

"*Vamanos*," Javier whispers. "Let's go."

But you're afraid you'll get shot if you run. You stand there, frozen. You and your family are rounded up in trucks. From there, you're packed tightly into a train car. You are deported and let out in the remote Mexican desert.

You have family in Mexico, but they don't live anywhere near here. You are stranded. You have no money and no means of transportation.

You are an American citizen. But the country of your birth has turned its back on you. In this moment, you vow never to go back.

It won't be easy, but you'll make a new life here in Mexico. You have no other choice.

THE END

To follow another path, turn to page 9.
To learn more about surviving the Great Depression, turn to page 99.

You'd love to catch up to your family. You already miss them. But making money is the whole reason you're here. You can't resist an opportunity like this, so you head south. It takes two days to make it to the farm. But once you arrive, you get a warm welcome.

An avocado field

"We've been expecting you," says the boss of the operation. "Hank speaks highly of you. We've got a big crew, and I need you to take charge."

The pay is good, and the farm is huge. You spend almost three weeks, earning more than you've ever made at one job. Soon, the word gets around. You're in demand. Over the next few months, you move from farm to farm, helping run operations. Time after time, people tell you to come back next year.

You've found success in the most difficult of conditions. It's lonely, and you miss your family. But you'll see them when you return to Mexico. And maybe next year, you can bring them with you to these new jobs. For the first time in years, your future looks brighter.

THE END

To follow another path, turn to page 9.
To learn more about surviving the Great Depression, turn to page 99.

CHAPTER 5

SURVIVING THE GREAT DEPRESSION

The 1920s were a booming time for the economy in the United States and across the world. After the bloody years of World War I (1914–1918), peace had led to prosperity. The decade was nicknamed "the Roaring Twenties." During that time the stock market soared. But all of that changed in 1929.

Factory workers in the 1920s pose for a company photo.

In September, stock prices began to drop. There were many reasons. Low wages for workers, agricultural problems, and mismanagement of money by banks were among the big ones. Investors began to realize that many stocks were overpriced. As stock owners began to sell their shares, the market started to dip.

On Thursday, October 24, that dip turned into a full dive. On a day that became known as Black Thursday, the stock market crashed. Over the next week, investors panicked as the crash continued.

By the time it was over, stocks were worth a fraction of their earlier value. People lost countless millions of dollars in the collapse. Many companies went out of business, and unemployment rose.

The effects of the collapse were felt around the globe. The Great Depression had begun. For almost ten years, the world economy was in shambles.

On its own, the collapse of the stock market would have been a disaster. But around the same time, an environmental crisis was making matters worse. In a large portion of America, decades of overfarming had left the topsoil thin and weak. Native plants had been cleared to make way for crops. Unlike the native plants, these new crops did little to hold the soil in place. So when drought hit, wind simply picked up the loose, dry soil and carried it off in great clouds.

The Dust Bowl left once productive farmland unable to support crops. Farms failed. People from Texas to Nebraska fled west in search of work. These migrant farmers were often called "Okies," since many came from Oklahoma.

A migrant family lives in a tent made with their car.

More than 200,000 people turned to this lifestyle to get by. Often, there were more workers than jobs. Employers offered little pay for farmwork.

Many migrant workers lived in simple shelters in temporary towns filled with wood and metal shacks. People faced poor sanitation, extreme poverty, food insecurity, and crime. Widespread racism made life even harder for people of color.

The Dust Bowl ended in the late 1930s. The dry weather patterns gave way to greater rainfall, and the erosion slowed down. But the damage was done. Many workers returned to their home states to reclaim the land. Farmers learned what and when to plant in order to help hold the soil in place.

The Great Depression officially lasted until 1939. However, the worst effects of it eased as early as 1933. That's the year President Franklin D. Roosevelt enacted legislation called the New Deal. It was designed to provide work for the masses of unemployed people.

Many people who had worked as migrants found work through the New Deal. Slowly but surely, the nation pulled itself out of the deepest depths of the Great Depression.

The economy further rebounded in 1941. That year, the United States entered World War II (1939–1945). The nation mobilized in the war effort. Factories pumped out tanks, planes, guns, and anything else needed in the war effort. The economy boomed. Hundreds of thousands of men went off to war. Women, who had been traditionally left out of the workforce, stepped in to do work that men had always done.

The Great Depression and the Dust Bowl were over. But the hard economic times left a lasting mark on the nation, as well as the people who lived through them. Millions of Americans who had suffered embraced new ideas of self-sufficiency. These ideas shaped American culture and were handed down to future generations.

Timeline of the Great Depression

1920–1929: The "Roaring Twenties" are a time of incredible economic growth. Stock markets surge. Many Americans—especially the wealthy—thrive. However, wages for working-class people remain low.

September 1929: Stock markets begin to dip. It signals more trouble to come.

October 1929: The stock market crashes. It marks the beginning of the Great Depression.

1930: Drought and overfarming lead to rapid erosion of topsoil in America's South-central and Midwest regions. Winds kick up huge clouds of dust.

1931–1933: Because of failing crops, ten percent of Oklahoma farmers lose their lands. Many head west to California in search of farmwork. They're called Okies—a term that soon comes to describe any displaced American farmer in search of work.

1933: President Franklin D. Roosevelt passes his New Deal. Over the next six years, the program provides jobs for thousands of unemployed workers.

April 14, 1935: The biggest dust storm of the Dust Bowl begins in Oklahoma. An estimated three million tons of topsoil is blown away in a massive black cloud. The event is called Black Sunday.

1939: Author John Steinbeck publishes *The Grapes of Wrath*. The novel tells the story of Okies struggling to live through the Dust Bowl and Great Depression. That same year, the Great Depression ends.

1941: The United States enters World War II. The war costs millions of lives, but it also kick-starts the economy. Factories produce weapons and supplies for the war effort.

Other Paths to Explore

1. Most migrant workers were men. At the time, many people did not believe women were well suited for hard farmwork. What would it be like to live as a woman in a shantytown? How might you help the family earn money? What would it be like to raise a family in those poor conditions?

2. Farmers who relied on migrant workers had difficult choices to make. Food prices were down. They weren't making as much money for their crops. And because there were so many workers, they could offer less pay. How would you feel hiring people at wages that were barely enough to survive on? Would you pay more, even when you were struggling yourself?

3. Politicians scrambled to find solutions during the Great Depression. What would it be like to work in Congress, or even the White House, while so many Americans were struggling? Would you see it as the government's job to pass laws to grow the economy? Or would you have looked for other solutions and let the economy repair itself naturally?

Bibliography

Enciso, Fernando Saul Alanis. *They Should Stay There: The Story of Mexican Migration and Repatriation During the Great Depression.* Chapel Hill, NC: The University of North Carolina Press, 2017.

History.com: The Dust Bowl
history.com/topics/great-depression/dust-bowl

PBS: Surviving the Dust Bowl
pbs.org/wgbh/americanexperience/films/dustbowl/

Smithsonian American Art Museum: The Great Okie Migration
americanexperience.si.edu/wp-content/uploads/2015/02/
The-Great-Okie-Migration.pdf

Glossary

dehydration (dee-hy-DRAY-shuhn)—a condition in which the body does not have enough water to function

deport (dee-PORT)—the act of sending illegal immigrants back to their own country

depression (di-PRE-shuhn)—a period during which business, jobs, and stock values stay low

economy (i-KAH-nuh-mee)—the ways in which a country handles its money and resources

erosion (i-ROH-zhuhn)—the wearing away of land by water or wind

heat stroke (HEET STROHK)—a serious illness caused by working in the heat too long

migrant worker (MY-gruht WER-ker)—a person who travels from place to place, looking for work

shantytown (SHAN-tee-town)—a temporary gathering of poorly built shacks and tents used by migrant workers during the Great Depression

shares (SHARES)—the small parts into which a company's stock is divided

stock market (STOCK MAHR-kit)—a place where stocks are bought and sold; someone who owns a stock owns part of a company

topsoil (TOP-soyl)—the top layer of soil that is best for planting

Read More

Berglund, Bruce R. *The Black Sunday Dust Blizzard: A Day that Changed America*. North Mankato, MN: Capstone Press, 2023.

Gitlin, Marty. *The Great Depression*. Ann Arbor, MI: Cherry Lake Publishing Group, 2022.

Smith, Elliott. *Focus on the Great Depression*. Minneapolis: Lerner Publications 2023.

Internet Sites

History for Kids: The Great Depression
historyforkids.org/the-great-depression/

Kids Discover: The Great Depression
online.kidsdiscover.com/unit/great-depression

US History: The Great Depression
ducksters.com/history/us_1900s/great_depression.php

JOIN OTHER HISTORICAL ADVENTURES WITH MORE
YOU CHOOSE SEEKING HISTORY!

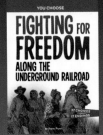
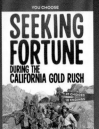

About the Author

Matt Doeden is a freelance author and editor from Minnesota. He's written numerous children's books on sports, music, current events, the military, extreme survival, and much more. Doeden began his career as a sports writer before turning to publishing. He lives in Minnesota with his wife and two children.